D0506803

17463

**Siskiyou County
Office of Education Library**
609 South Gold Street
Yreka, CA   96097

Visual Geography Series®

NIGERIA

...in Pictures

Prepared by
Geography Department

Lerner Publications Company
Minneapolis   17463

Copyright © 1988 by Lerner Publications Company

All rights reserved. International copyright secured. No part of this book may be reproduced, stored in a retrieval system, or transmitted in any form or by any means—electronic, mechanical, photocopying, recording, or otherwise—without the prior written permission of the publisher, except for the inclusion of brief quotations in an acknowledged review.

Independent Picture Service

Intricately sculpted walls adorn a clay building in a northern city.

This is an all-new edition of the Visual Geography Series. Previous editions have been published by Sterling Publishing Company, New York City, and some of the original textual information has been retained. New photographs, maps, charts, captions, and updated information have been added. The text has been entirely reset in 10/12 Century Textbook.

LIBRARY OF CONGRESS CATALOGING-IN-PUBLICATION DATA

Nigeria in pictures.

(Visual geography series)
Rev. ed. of: Nigeria in pictures / prepared by John Schultz.
Includes index.
Summary: Introduces the land, history, government, people, and economy of Nigeria.
1. Nigeria. [1. Nigeria] I. Schultz, John Frederick, 1944- . Nigeria in pictures. II. Lerner Publications Company. Geography Dept. III. Series: Visual geography series (Minneapolis, Minn.)
DT515.22.N55   1988   966.9   87–17267
ISBN 0-8225-1826-0 (lib. bdg.)

International Standard Book Number: 0-8225-1826-0
Library of Congress Catalog Card Number: 87-17267

VISUAL GEOGRAPHY SERIES®

Publisher
Harry Jonas Lerner
Associate Publisher
Nancy M. Campbell
Senior Editor
Mary M. Rodgers
Editor
Gretchen Bratvold
Illustrations Editor
Karen A. Sirvaitis
Consultants/Contributors
Thomas O'Toole
Sandra K. Davis
Designer
Jim Simondet
Cartographer
Carol F. Barrett
Indexer
Sylvia Timian
Production Manager
Richard J. Hannah

Independent Picture Service

To protect himself from the strong savanna sun, a Hausa farmer wears a broad-brimmed straw hat.

Acknowledgments

Title page photo courtesy of Yosef Hadar, World Bank Photo.

Elevation contours adapted from *The Times Atlas of the World,* seventh comprehensive edition (New York: Times Books, 1985).

2 3 4 5 6 7 8 9 10 97 96 95 94 93 92 91 90 89

Photo by Jim Hathaway

A museum in Kano typifies the traditional Hausa architecture of northern Nigeria. The walls were built of mud at the beginning of the dry season so they would bake and harden in the sun.

Contents

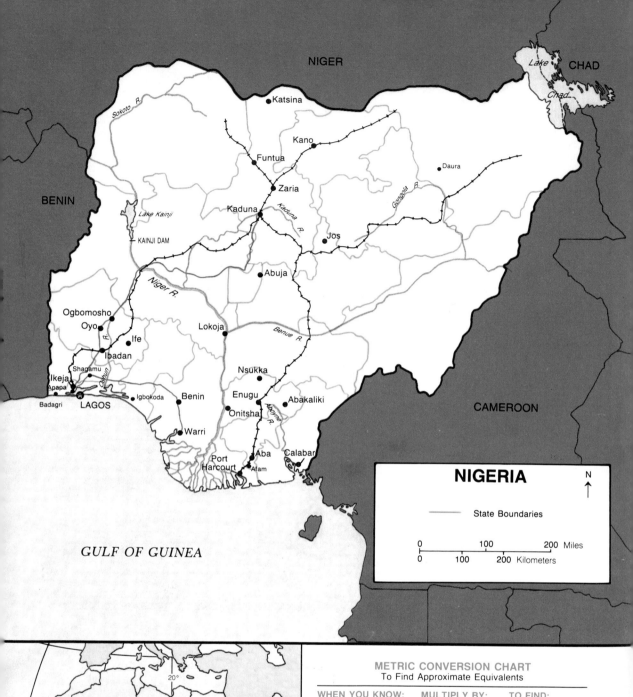

NIGER

Katsina

Kano

Funtua

Zaria

Daura

Kaduna

Sokoto R.

Kaduna R.

Gongola R.

Jos

Lake Kainji

KAINJI DAM

BENIN

Abuja

Niger R.

Ogbomosho

Oyo

Ife

Ibadan

Shagamu

Ikeja

Apapa

Badagri

LAGOS

Igbokoda

Benin

Warri

Lokoja

Benue R.

Nsukka

Enugu

Onitsha

Abakaliki

Anambra R.

Port
Harcourt

Aba

Afam

Calabar

CAMEROON

Lake
Chad

Chad

CHAD

GULF OF GUINEA

NIGERIA

N

— State Boundaries

0	100	200 Miles
0	100	200 Kilometers

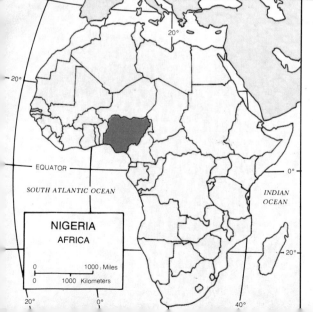

20°

20°

EQUATOR

SOUTH ATLANTIC OCEAN

INDIAN
OCEAN

0°

20°

NIGERIA
AFRICA

0	1000 Miles
0	1000 Kilometers

20°   0°   40°

METRIC CONVERSION CHART
To Find Approximate Equivalents

WHEN YOU KNOW:	MULTIPLY BY:	TO FIND:
AREA		
acres	0.41	hectares
square miles	2.59	square kilometers
CAPACITY		
gallons	3.79	liters
LENGTH		
feet	30.48	centimeters
yards	0.91	meters
miles	1.61	kilometers
MASS (weight)		
pounds	0.45	kilograms
tons	0.91	metric tons
VOLUME		
cubic yards	0.77	cubic meters
TEMPERATURE		
degrees Fahrenheit	0.56 (*after* subtracting 32)	degrees Celsius

An oil tanker transports petroleum from an offshore oil well. Petroleum production, which accounts for over 90 percent of Nigeria's export revenues, has fallen sharply in recent years, causing a reduction in oil income and an economic slump.

Photo by Texaco Inc.

Introduction

Nigeria—perhaps more than any other nation in Africa—has the potential to become the most influential country on the continent. If its present birth rate continues, the country may also soon become the world's third most-populous country (after China and India). One out of every four black Africans lives in Nigeria, and the country is a dominant force in the political and economic life of the continent.

Fueled by the profits of their country's oil industry, Nigerians have developed

5

exceptional systems of transportation and communication, funneling sophisticated technology and business methods toward a willing and eager population. Many dirt roads are now paved, and local radio stations and television channels beam messages even into some relatively remote villages. Improving literacy rates have made Nigerians receptive to international ideas, as well as to innovations in technology and business.

Yet Nigeria is not an evenly developed country. Many areas have not benefited from the profits of the oil industry. Furthermore, since 1973, the oil profits have diminished at an alarming rate. The country's economic system, which first had to adjust to independence and a civil war, has had to readjust to falling revenues. Farmers and wage earners are suffering from inflation and devaluation—a decrease in the exchange value of their money. The efficient systems of communication remain in place, reminding Nigerians of all the things they do not have. The resulting frustrations have led to an era of political uncertainty.

Nigerians have struggled hard for political solutions to their problems. Parliamentary democracy, installed by the British in 1960, soon gave way to military governments and civil war. A U.S.-style democracy attempted in 1979 collapsed in 1983. The military remains in charge—they claim as a temporary solution—until a new political system can be devised. In the meantime, Nigerians have accepted military rule very reluctantly.

Despite recent difficulties, however, the vast potential for growth remains. Nigeria is a nation of abundant natural resources and of educated, energetic people who embrace a global outlook. Many Nigerians have traveled abroad, returning with a wealth of new economic and political ideas. As Nigeria moves toward a more prosperous future, it could lead the rest of Africa along similar paths.

Courtesy of Angene Wilson

The administration building of Ahmadu Bello University in Zaria—one of Nigeria's 12 universities—reflects a modern architectural style. An educated population will be important for Nigeria's future success.

Photo by Jim Hathaway

In the high plains of western Ondo state, many steep, isolated rock domes—called inselbergs—are left standing by the erosion of the surrounding terrain. They rise sharply to mounds of up to 3,000 feet above sea level.

1) The Land

Nigeria is located on the Gulf of Guinea, where West and Central Africa meet. Encompassing diverse environments, Nigeria's land ranges from the Sahara Desert in the north to coastal swamps along the Gulf of Guinea in the south. With 356,699 square miles, the country is more than twice the size of the state of California.

The nation is bounded on three sides by former French-dominated nations—Benin to the west, Niger to the north, and Cameroon to the east. Its 500-mile southern border fronts on the Atlantic Ocean. The northeast corner of Nigeria borders on Lake Chad, which lies mostly in Chad.

Topography

Compared to the rugged terrain of eastern and southern Africa, the physical features of Nigeria are modest in scale. Much of the country's surface is formed by a group of extensive plateaus and high plains. On these broad plains, distinctive hills and rocky domes, called inselbergs, emerge on the landscape. More impressive highlands

7

and volcanic hills appear near the eastern border and on the Jos Plateau, which rises over 6,000 feet in the middle of the country. The valleys of the Niger and Benue rivers separate these expansive northern plains from the southern lowlands, which do not exceed an elevation of 1,000 feet above sea level.

Because of the relatively low, uniform shape of the land, the climatic and vegetation zones in the country are quite regular from south to north. Five distinct bands can be distinguished, as the swamps and dense forests of the south give way northward to more open savanna landscapes. Within these bands, or ecological zones, characteristic flora and fauna, as well as human cultural adaptations to the environment, are found in distinctive settings. The regions are the coastal zone, the rainforest belt, the Guinea Savanna, the Sudan Savanna, and the Sahel.

The Coastal Zone

In the creeks and mangrove swamps of the Niger River Delta and the lagoon coast, rainfall exceeds 100 inches per year. For most of this southernmost zone, sandy beaches are backed by a belt of swampland that, in places, extends up to 60 miles inland. The saltwater or mangrove swamp belt is largely a maze of islands among countless creeks and streams. Early explorers regarded this zone as an obstacle that they could not penetrate, and it still forms a barrier to shipping. A strong current off the coast creates sandbars that block the entrances to ports unless they are dredged continually.

Coconut palms abound in this coastal area, while farther inland, away from the influence of tidal waters, the raffia palm is common and is tapped for sap to make palm wine. Another valuable tree is the oil palm, long commercially important for the oil extracted from its fleshy fruit. In the mid-twentieth century the Niger Delta entered a second oil age. Today numerous petroleum fields dot the region, in addition to the trees that produce palm oil.

Courtesy of Ruth Karl

Industrious ants shaped a huge anthill out of mud in the southern tropical rain-forest. Many large insects thrive in Nigeria.

Photo by Jim Hathaway

Palm trees grow abundantly in the low, sandy coastal belt, which gives way to swamps, marshes, and jungle farther inland.

Toads and frogs, river turtles, water snakes, and, occasionally, a crocodile or hippopotamus can be found in this creek and mangrove area. The manatee—a huge aquatic mammal—feeds on underwater plants in the delta area. Many different types of shore birds, such as sandpipers, herons, and whimbrels, are a common sight.

The earliest inhabitants of the coastal zone were fishing and river-dwelling peoples who traveled the area in dugout canoes. They tended to live in scattered and isolated groups. Small villages were built on stilts above the water. Larger coastal settlements, such as Badagri and

Calabar, developed when the coast thrived on the slave and palm oil trade. But because of the comparatively inhospitable environment, this zone remained sparsely populated until recent times.

The Rain-Forest

North of the coastal area, the tropical rain-forest encompasses an 80-mile-wide belt that covers less than 20 percent of the country. This area is tangled with dense undergrowth and is thickly forested with trees that measure as much as 100 feet in height. In its untouched form, the rain-forest can block sunlight from reaching the ground. Many of these trees—such as mahogany, iroko, and obeche—provide valuable hardwood. Rainfall in the area averages 60 to 80 inches annually.

The growth of Nigeria's population has greatly reduced the size and density of these humid rain-forests. Within the last century rubber trees and oil palms have replaced many of the wild species. Cacao trees—from which chocolate is obtained—are heavily planted in the western part of this zone, and cacao beans are Nigeria's second major export after petroleum oil. A region around Shagamu produces most of

Cacao trees are plentiful in Nigeria's rain-forests. The pods hanging from the tree are picked and broken open to extract the cacao beans, which are eventually made into chocolate.

Independent Picture Service

Independent Picture Service

South of the rain-forest, along the coast near Lagos, fishermen return with their catch at the end of the day. The selection of coastal fish includes sardines and mackerel.

the nation's kola nuts, which many Nigerians chew as a stimulant and which are an ingredient in Coca-Cola.

Tree- and ground-dwelling animals are found in abundance in this ecological zone. Lizards, monkeys, chimpanzees, and squirrels are common, as are geckos, chameleons, and fruit bats. The rain-forest contains an abundance of bird life. Hawks and hornbills, the West African touraco (a red-winged cousin of the cuckoo), and the African gray parrot are among the species seen most frequently. Some creatures harmful to humans also inhabit this zone —for example, army ants march through the region, and other bothersome insects thrive in the area, as do a few poisonous snakes.

In the past, settlements in this region— especially in the east—were widely dispersed because of the thick rain-forest. The difficulty involved in clearing the dense vegetation required that large communal work teams farm the land. In addition, a type of agriculture evolved that was very different from the large-scale method of planting huge fields with a single crop. Instead, farmers chose to preserve the great diversity of species in the rain-forest by planting a large variety of tree and root crops throughout the forest.

The Guinea Savanna

In this transitional belt of woodland mixed with tall grasses, rainfall averages 40 to 60 inches per year, although four to five months receive less than 1 inch of rain. Broadleafed, deciduous (leaf-shedding) trees that rise up to 40 feet high tower above long grasses and shrubs. Most of the trees, such as the baobab, are fire-

11

Photo by Jim Hathaway

Covering an area of about 3,000 square miles, the Jos Plateau is separated from the surrounding plains by steep cliffs. Some hills on the plateau tower to heights of over 5,800 feet, and temperatures on the plateau are considerably cooler than in surrounding regions.

resistant and have twisted trunks. As in most savanna regions of Africa, much of this zone is burned year after year—usually intentionally. Farmers may light fires to clear land or to improve the soil with ash. Hunters may use fire to drive game into traps. Frequently, the savanna is fired to prevent its burning out of control during the height of the dry season.

This thinly populated central region comprises 40 percent of the area of Nigeria but contains only 20 percent of the population. A number of small settlements are clustered among the rocky hills on the northern side of the Benue River. Because the soil in this region is of poor quality, it has never been a prime agricultural area.

One subregion within the Guinea Savanna stands out in contrast to its surroundings. The Jos Plateau rises to over 6,000 feet in places, which affects its climate. The vegetation on the plateau consists mostly of grasslands. Unlike the rest of the region, the Jos Plateau is overpopulated, probably because it served as a haven for refugees in the past and because of the mineral resources found in the area.

The Sudan Savanna

The Sudan Savanna—which extends across north central Africa south of the Sahara and Libyan deserts—forms the heartland of northern Nigeria. Rainfall averages 20 to 40 inches annually, with seven nearly rainless months. One of the most distinctive zones in terms of climate, vegetation, and people, this area is also one of the most productive regions in the country.

Independent Picture Service

Small, white cattle egrets befriend cattle or buffalo by eating insects off their skin and by warning them of approaching enemies.

Trees such as the baobab and the doom palm grow singly in a scattered pattern. The doom palm is also known as the gingerbread palm because of the taste of its edible, fibrous fruit. Large expanses of short grasslands and scrub are common. Much of this zone has an open, parkland appearance where carob, shea, and ceiba trees are grown and protected because of their crop-producing value to farmers. Smaller acacia trees are found in the northern reaches.

Gazelles and other antelope graze the grasslands in a few areas of the Sudan Savanna. An occasional hyena or leopard may be found outside the forest reserves in this zone. Small mammals—rats, hares, hedgehogs, and monkeys—abound. Bird life is also plentiful—cranes, parrots, and rollers are seen, but more common are cattle egrets and scavengers such as vultures.

Large populations—supported by farming on the lighter and generally more fertile soil of the region—are clustered around the old, walled cities of this zone. Peanut, cotton, and tobacco production have expanded considerably in recent decades. Grains such as millet, sorghum, and maize (corn) grow well in the area and are the dominant food crops.

The Sahel

The northernmost zone, which occupies only the fringes of Nigeria and the Lake Chad Basin, receives far less rainfall than the rest of the country, usually less than 20 inches per year. Characteristic vegetation consists of acacias and other thorny shrubs. Sheep, cattle, and camels graze on the short, wiry grasses. Fires are less frequent here than farther south because there are not enough trees to fuel them or people to start them.

Although a somewhat more hostile environment than the savanna to the south,

Courtesy of Eliot Elisofon, Eliot Elisofon Archives, National Museum of African Art, Smithsonian Institution

The Benue River joins the Niger, which changes course near Lokoja to flow south toward the Gulf of Guinea. The combined valleys of the Niger and Benue rivers form a large west-east arc across the middle of the country.

the Sahel zone has supported farming and animal raising for a long time. Crop failure and water shortages are a common feature of life, and people have learned to accept them. Experts speculate that the Sahara Desert is spreading southward into this region—marked by the slow advance of sand and the decrease in the amount of moisture in the soil.

Rivers and Lakes

Originating outside the country, the Niger —from which Nigeria takes its name—and the Benue rivers are the leading interior waterways. The Benue flows into the Niger at Lokoja, where the enlarged waterway continues to the Gulf of Guinea via a network of tributaries that form huge deltas. Unlike many African rivers, the Niger and the Benue are navigable for long stretches during most of the year. All of the rivers north of the Lokoja begin in the Jos Plateau. These include the Sokoto, the Kaduna—named for the crocodiles it

once held—and the Gongola rivers, as well as several waterways that drain into Lake Chad.

Lake Chad itself is a vast expanse of shallow water in the northeast, with most of its shores outside Nigeria. With a maximum depth of about 23 feet, Lake Chad is the shallowest lake of its size in the world. Its underwater area varies from about 4,000 to 10,000 square miles, depending on the season of the year. In recent years the lake has receded considerably. The only other large body of water in the country is man-made Lake Kainji, formed by the damming of the Niger in western Nigeria.

Climate

Situated well within the tropics, Nigeria has temperatures that remain relatively high throughout the year. The average temperature ranges from 65° F to 87° F in the south and from 73° F to 95° F in the north.

Independent Picture Service

A fisherman casts his net in Lake Kainji. Construction of the dam at Kainji was completed in 1968 and created a lake covering some 750 square miles. The new lake forced the evacuation of 42,000 people to over 100 new villages.

In a parched area of northern Nigeria, a mother and daughter find a barren patch of dried earth where a water hole once stood. Drought poses a constant threat in northern Nigeria, where extremely low levels of rainfall cause the water supply to evaporate during the dry season.

Courtesy of CARE

In contrast to the four seasons in Europe and the United States, most of Nigeria has two distinct climatic periods—a wet season and a dry season. The length of the rainy season is governed by the movement of the intertropical convergence zone, which is the name given to a meeting point of air-pressure systems. The rain may start in January in the south and move progressively northward, reaching the northern regions by April. Thus, the length of the rainy season varies from nearly 12 months on the coast to less than 5 months inland. During the dry season in the north, a strong, dust-laden wind called the harmattan blows from the desert. The wind produces a haze that covers the northernmost areas in December and January and that usually reduces temperatures considerably.

Natural Resources

Nigeria holds a leading position among African nations in mineral and energy resources. Tin from the Jos Plateau has long been the mainstay of mining in the country. Much of the world's columbite, a mineral byproduct of the tin mines, is also produced in the Jos region. Important lead and zinc deposits are located near Abakaliki, and iron ore is found in several places. Nigeria also has quantities of gold, manganese, and other minerals.

Oil is the leading export from Nigeria. Since 1980, this sector of the Nigerian economy has suffered a serious decline, with production decreasing by about one-third. Proven reserves are high—more than 16 billion barrels—but Nigeria's oil fields are small in comparison with those of other African nations, such as Libya

15

and Algeria. Natural gas exists in great quantities. A large power station using natural gas was built at Afam, and another complex is planned.

Cities

Unlike most African nations in which a single main city serves as the economic center of the nation, Nigeria has a number of cities with populations that exceed one million people. Some of these have a centuries-old history. Others have been developed in recent decades as farm workers have arrived in search of industrial jobs, attracted by the possibility of a better life in the cities. For the most part, the cities have not been able to keep pace with their excessive growth rate. Shantytowns with no sanitation facilities can be seen alongside ultramodern, air-conditioned skyscrapers.

THE CAPITAL

The island city of Lagos, known locally as Eko, was founded more than 300 years ago by a subgroup of the Yoruba, who found the site easy to defend. As the capital of the nation, the city has mushroomed out of all proportion to its capacity. One of the fastest-growing cities in the world, Lagos is a combination of urban excitement and urban blight. The government has attempted to build a new capital at Abuja to relieve some of the pressures on the inhabitants of Lagos, who number nearly five million. Lack of funds, however, has delayed completion of this project.

The main port district of Lagos is Apapa, which lies on the mainland and handles nearly 70 percent of Nigeria's international trade. Lagos also has the greatest concentration of industry in the country and is a major commercial and administrative hub. Yet the city is as well

Photo by Carol Barker

As Nigeria's political capital, leading port, commercial center, and largest city, Lagos teems with activity. Among the most congested cities in Africa, it is full of people, vehicles, and every type of dwelling, from shanty to skyscraper.

16

Courtesy of Phillip S. Stevens, Jr., Eliot Elisofon Archives, National Museum of African Art, Smithsonian Institution

A small village on an inlet of the Niger River offers an alternative to the overcrowding of Nigeria's many cities. Even in rural areas, overpopulation presents problems. Nigeria has the largest population of any country In Africa, and it is still increasing rapidly.

An informal market lines a narrow street in Kano. The city's long-established reputation as a trading center stems from the local production of dyed leather and woven cloth.

Photo by Phil Porter

17

Located in Oshogbo, a town near the Oshun River, this carved, concrete archway serves as the entrance to a shrine honoring the Yoruba goddess Oshun. Every year a festival is held to worship the goddess.

Photo by Jim Hathaway

known for its vibrant nightlife as it is for its commerce. Cinemas, cabarets, casinos, and sidewalk meeting places are active long after offices close.

SECONDARY CITIES

Ibadan, 85 miles north of Lagos, was originally a hilly fortress city built during the Yoruba Wars against Dahomey (present-day Benin) in the nineteenth century. Although it has swelled into a sprawling metropolis of four or five million people, Ibadan is, like many of the Yoruba towns, still an agricultural market city. Many people who live in the city commute daily to their nearby farms. Ibadan is the home of one of the most highly respected university campuses in Africa, as well as some of the worst slums.

Kano is the principal northern commercial city and the capital of Kano state. For centuries, the great caravans that crossed West Africa set out from Kano. Now, with an airport and a railway to the south, it remains a center of international exchange. Kano is really two cities—an old and a new settlement. Its old walled town, the Tsohon Gari, represents 1,000 years of domination by the Hausa—the largest eth-

nic group in Nigeria. An attractive mosque (Islamic house of worship) and the 800-year-old Emir's Palace rise above bustling, traditional marketplaces. Adjacent to the walled city is the new, modern city, with its Sabon Gari sector where non-Hausa Nigerians have traditionally resided.

Kaduna, a relatively new city, was built in 1912 to serve as the capital of Kaduna state and is an administrative and communications hub for much of the north. Kaduna is an example of city planning, a rarity among Nigeria's towns. Dignified suburban housing developments and carefully laid-out thoroughfares reveal Kaduna's newness. Unlike many other northern cities, its more than 500,000 residents come from all corners of the country and represent many ethnic and social backgrounds.

Nigeria boasts a number of other large cities, each with a distinctive character. Benin clings to the ancient royal tradition depicted in its famous bronzes. The artists and craftspeople of Oshogbo maintain forest shrines to the protecting Oshun river spirit. Zaria thrives as an educational city, and Onitsha has rebuilt its gigantic market following the civil war of the 1960s.

Courtesy of Ruth Karl

The decorative terraces of this hotel in Ibadan reflect Brazilian style, which was introduced into Nigeria by members of the Yoruba who had been sent to Brazil as slaves. After gaining freedom, some of them returned to their homeland, bringing Brazilian influence to Nigeria.

2) History and Government

Nigeria's present boundaries were drawn in 1914. Although the country was created because of European ambitions and rivalries in West Africa, its peoples had a rich history before the colonial borders were defined. The newly created nation contained a number of great kingdoms that had developed complex systems of government completely independent of Europe.

Ancient Heritage

For thousands of years humans have lived in the area that is now known as Nigeria. More than 2,000 years ago a technically sophisticated culture evolved in the Nok Valley, an area that extended west and south of the Jos Plateau. The valley is surrounded by rocks containing sedimentary deposits of tin. Perhaps attracted by this

Courtesy of Ruth Karl

Yoruba masks are shaded in colors that artists prepare from leaves, seeds, wood, and various earth pigments. Those who carve masks and figurines are considered carvers of art, while those who make practical objects, such as bowls, are referred to as carvers of wood.

important trade item, people settled in the area and created a culture best known for its terra-cotta (baked clay) figurines and iron artifacts.

NORTHERN KINGDOMS

The northern cities of Kano, Katsina, and others were founded by Hausa-speaking peoples after about A.D. 1000, and the earliest origins of the great Kanem-Bornu Empire around Lake Chad date back even further. Between 1100 and 1500 Kanem-Bornu was one of the major powers in the Sudan—a region that extended from Senegal to Ethiopia—rivaling the great empires of Ghana, Mali, and Songhai farther west. The advantages that helped these Sudanese kingdoms to evolve were similar. For example, the grasslands afforded easy movement of people and ideas. Furthermore, the position of the kingdoms astride the great trade routes gave the people an ideal location to serve as commercial go-betweens. From the south came

gold, slaves, and ivory; from the north, salt, cloth, horses, and metals.

Located around Lake Chad, the Kanuri and So peoples of the Kanem-Bornu Empire developed a centralized political system that collected taxes, raised armies, and regulated commerce. The greatest legacy of these states, however, was in their contacts with North Africa and with Islam —the religion based on the Koran (holy writings) and its interpretation by the prophet Muhammad. From the eleventh century onward, Muslims (followers of Islam) advanced across the land and exerted tremendous influence in the Sudanese grasslands.

Between the empires of Kanem-Bornu and Songhai lay the Hausa Bakwai—the seven city-states of Hausaland. Legend has it that a man named Bayajidda traveled from Baghdad to the Hausa city of Daura, where he killed a sacred snake that had prevented the people from using their well. In gratitude, the queen of Daura married him and bore him a son, Bawo. Bawo succeeded his father to the throne and had seven sons—Biram, Daura, Katsina, Zaria, Kano, Rano, and Gobir, each of whom became king of a city-state that bore his name.

By the fifteenth century, the fortified Hausa states were well known to the outside world. Struggles developed in Hausaland during the sixteenth century, both between city-states and from neighboring kingdoms. Prominent groups such as the Jukun from Kororofa were involved in continual rivalries and raids aimed at taxation and expansion.

SOUTHERN KINGDOMS

While the savanna offered the greatest opportunity for groups to form centralized states, the rain-forest retained village-level organizations for a much longer time. Yet the development of the Yoruba domains of Oyo, Benin, and Dahomey proved that people could overcome the barrier of the forest belt and establish states within the rain-forest.

The city of Ife was the focal point of Yoruba spiritual life, and its *oni* (kings) were religious leaders. The Yoruba peoples of the southwest have a creation myth that talks of Ife as the origin of life. The Oyo, a subgroup of the Yoruba, developed the most powerful empire. According to tradition, the Oyo Empire was founded in the late fourteenth century by Oranmiyan, who transferred political power from Ife to the city of Oyo. At its height, the Oyo Empire covered a huge area from the Niger River to the frontier of modern Togo. Another great realm from the same period was Benin. A strong, well-organized state, Benin also was well situated to attract the Portuguese merchants who arrived in the fifteenth century.

Photo by Phil Porter

Agba ile, or elders, of the Oyo ethnic group often hold meetings to discuss community issues, such as the collection of taxes.

21

Independent Picture Service

Tuareg camel riders customarily make their home in the Sahara Desert far north of Nigeria, only coming into the country for short periods to work as watchkeepers and guards in the cities. Drought conditions in the 1970s, however, forced many Tuareg families to travel south, where some still remain.

Independent Picture Service

Constructed entirely of mud and timber, this Muslim-style house features rainspouts that carry off the torrential downpours of the rainy season.

Atlantic Slave Trade

Until the arrival of Europeans in the fifteenth century, the coast had little significance in the politics of West Africa. All of the great empires, such as Oyo and Benin, looked to the interior for trade. But once the Portuguese established a settlement on the nearby island of São Tomé in the Gulf of Guinea, they discovered that the Benin peoples could supply one of their greatest needs—a low-cost work force. Later, the Europeans realized that huge profits could be made by exporting blacks from Benin to work as slaves at the gold fields along the Gold Coast in present-day Ghana. Thus began one of the most remarkable forced migrations in history. The whole pattern of the world's population was altered.

Initially, Benin prospered during the slaving era. But soon its provinces fell into chaos from the effects of slavery raids and wars with other communities. The em-

22

pire crumbled. The very commercial life on which its strength had been built became its greatest weakness once slaves from Benin became the primary commodity of the trade.

For four centuries the slave trade dominated relations between the peoples of Nigeria and the peoples of Europe and the Americas. European colonization of the Americas provided a massive new demand for labor. The sale of Africans by other Africans had been common for centuries, and European merchants took advantage of this practice to make their own profits. This transatlantic commerce in human cargo had profound effects on Europe, the New World, and Africa.

The slave trade spread Nigerians widely throughout the globe. Many of the

Courtesy of Eliot Elisofon, Eliot Elisofon Archives, National Museum of African Art, Smithsonian Institution

Islamic influence is found in this illustration of a lancer in the army of the sultan of Begharmi. *Sultan* is derived from an Arabic word meaning "authority."

Courtesy of Library of Congress

Africans sent to the New World were crowded onto ships until they filled every available space. Many of those who became ill during the long journey were thrown overboard, still bound in chains, to drown.

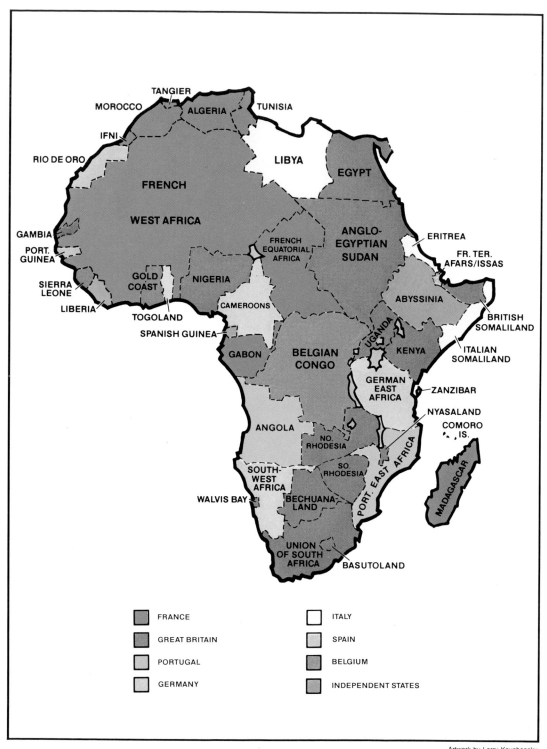

Artwork by Larry Kaushansky

By the late nineteenth century European powers had carved the continent of Africa into areas of influence. Present-day Nigeria was included in the holdings claimed by Great Britain. Map information taken from *The Anchor Atlas of World History*, 1978.

Nigerians who were forcibly settled in the New World soon lost their ethnic identities. The Yoruba, in contrast, frequently preserved their cultural heritage. A large group of Yoruba slaves revolted in Brazil in the 1800s, for example, and were sent back to Nigeria. The distinctive, Brazilian-style homes these people built upon their return can still be found in Lagos.

Nineteenth-Century Turmoil

Three factors combined to transform the Nigerian scene in the nineteenth century. These factors were the Muslim jihads (holy wars) and Yoruba civil wars, European exploration and missionary efforts, and a revolution in trade.

A Muslim reform movement, conducted mainly by the Fulbé people of the north, was inspired by an Islamic scholar named Usman Dan Fodio. The armies of the Dan Fodio jihad swept across the Hausa states. By 1830 the Fulbé were masters of most of the north and had defeated the Bornu

and Oyo empires as well. The breakdown of the authority of the king of Oyo led to 80 years of civil war in Yorubaland.

At the turn of the nineteenth century, Nigerians were largely free of European influence. By the end of the century, the arrival of European traders, soldiers, and missionaries had deeply affected Nigerian life. The British, as a result of the industrial revolution, were anxious to open African markets to their low-priced textiles and manufactured goods.

British merchants and their African partners found that profits in palm oil, which was used for making soap and as a lubricant for the textile machinery of Great Britain, were greater than those to be made in the slave trade. When African leaders sought to control the palm oil trade for their own benefit, the British used military force to monopolize the trade. Missionaries in the region—eager to reduce the slave trade—assisted by assuring the British people that this military occupation was beneficial to the Africans.

World Bank Photo

Men lay additional track onto one of Nigeria's railway lines. By the mid-1960s most railroad companies had replaced steam locomotives with diesel-powered engines.

British Occupation

Britain acquired the territory of Nigeria in stages. Its earliest spheres of influence were the crown colony of Lagos and the Oil Rivers Protectorate in the Niger Delta. In 1877 Sir George Goldie united British trading companies into a single firm, and the outlines of Nigeria began to emerge.

It was relatively easy for Britain to establish its claims through negotiation with the French and Germans. It was quite another matter to get Nigerian peoples to accept British rule. King Jaja of Opobo, for example, resisted British efforts to eliminate his role as a trade merchant. Sir Frederick Lugard, head of the West African Frontier Force, conquered the northern states between 1901 and 1906. In 1914 the Protectorates of Southern and Northern Nigeria were merged to form a single unit—the Colony and Protectorate of Nigeria.

Colonial Rule

The British created a huge trade area for Europeans that was free of African competition. They collected taxes from the Africans in European currency, which forced the Africans to sell goods to Europeans in order to have money for the tax. As a result, the demand for European goods also increased, since Africans had less time to produce cloth and other products for local markets.

To overcome a shortage of trained personnel and to limit expenses, the British instituted a system of indirect rule. Local Nigerian officials remained in power to administer the rulings of British colonial authorities. This system proved more successful in the north—where a similar system had been practiced for centuries—than in the south. In contrast, while missionaries dominated the educational system in the south and made rapid advances, they were restricted in the north where Islamic education remained dominant.

Changes came quite rapidly to Nigerian society as new transportation routes, such as a railway linking the north to the sea, were opened. Many Nigerians had served as soldiers in World War I, and a new, educated class of people was emerging. This new class began to think of themselves as Nigerians rather than simply as members of their local ethnic groups. Africanus Horton, born in Sierra Leone and educated at Edinburgh, Scotland, attacked the concept of African inferiority, which many of the British had used to justify their rule over blacks.

Independent Picture Service

This Hausa compound at Funtua combines contemporary materials with traditional style. At the base, the walls of the compound may be as much as three feet thick.

With support from the United Nations Special Fund, the Nigerian government established a training program for vocational instructors near Lagos. The grant also included funds to train foremen at Kaduna.

Courtesy of International Labor Office

By 1930 a growing number of Nigerians were expressing their discontent with foreign rule. Earlier, a revolt among the marketwomen at Aba had forced the local government to make reforms in the east. Herbert Macaulay became the spokesperson for anticolonial sentiments, and his party—the Nigerian National Democratic party—won all the Lagos seats in the Legislative Council in the 1939 elections.

The pace of advancement toward self-rule quickened. By 1949 the issue of autonomy was overshadowed by the question of how the powers given up by the British would be shared. Various constitutional conferences were held in Lagos and London from 1949 to 1960 to seek an acceptable framework of government.

Independence

Under the Constitution of 1954 Nigeria became a federation consisting of three regions (Northern, Western, and Eastern), with a federal capital at Lagos. The new document provided for a parliamentary system of government in which all men and women were eligible to vote. After the elections of 1959 and some hard political bargaining among factions, Nigeria achieved independence from the British government on October 1, 1960. Nigerians had won the right to govern themselves, and Nigeria became a member of the United Nations.

Although direct colonial rule had lasted only 60 years, the legacy of British colonialism left its mark on the nation. The effects of its presence are found in practically every aspect of Nigerian life, from its legal and educational systems to the use of English as the national language.

Upon gaining independence Nigeria had to deal with an economy still controlled by the British. In addition, the national government had to take steps to improve the

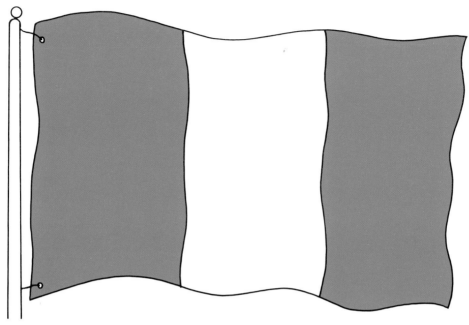

Artwork by Jim Simondet

The design for Nigeria's national flag was selected from among almost 3,000 submissions and was officially adopted in 1960. Two bands of green symbolize Nigerian agriculture – the mainstay of the national economy – and the white section in the middle signifies peace and unity.

educational system in order to expand the number of skilled workers.

The country's unity was tested shortly after gaining independence. In the Western Region, riots and political strife between ethnic groups broke out, forcing the federal government to take charge. A fourth region, the Midwest, was created to accommodate non-Yoruba minorities who had opposed being included in the Western Region. It became apparent during the political turmoil of the 1960s that grave weaknesses existed in the federal system of government.

Internal Tensions

Many Nigerians held more loyalty for their ethnic group or place of birth than for the new nation. The political parties that had operated while Nigeria was under a parliamentary system were lively and independent. Unfortunately, they were also divided along regional and ethnic lines.

The Northern Peoples Congress dominated politics in the north, the Action Group was strong in the west, and the National Council of Nigerian Citizens was favored in the east. The regional self-rule that was granted in the Constitution of 1954 strengthened ethnic interests. Large minority groups, such as the Tiv in the east, felt themselves dominated by outsiders. Regionally based, elective governments did not survive the pressure of conflicting ethnic groups. These tensions still influence the Nigerian scene.

The first Nigerian republic came to an end in 1966, when the military intervened in the government. Army officers removed corrupt politicians and tried to abolish the federal system of four regions. In response, ethnic rioting broke out in parts of the country. The fury of the north was directed against the Ibo, the target of long, pent-up jealousies. A second coup d'état brought a military regime to power, and the responsibility for holding Nigeria together fell to Colonel Yakubu Gowon, who was only 31 years old.

The constitutional crisis escalated, and in 1967 the Eastern Region separated from the nation and declared itself the independent Republic of Biafra. Eastern leaders felt alienated and did not want to share their expected oil revenues with the rest of the country. The disagreement caused the other groups to drop their differences and to rally to the defense of the federation. Consequently, fighting broke out.

The Civil War

The most significant feature of the civil war was its length. Like the Civil War in the United States, gallantry and brutality existed on both sides as brother and sister fought against brother and sister. Eventually, a great deal of international attention was put into humanitarian efforts to aid the Biafrans. The war ended abruptly in 1970—on the tenth anniversary of Nigeria's independence—when the leader of the Eastern Region, Colonel Odumegwu Ojukwu, fled and the Ibo surrendered.

Although increased revenues from the oil industry hastened Nigeria's recovery from the civil war, those living in urban slums saw no benefits. In addition, General Gowon kept postponing the promised return to civilian rule. Popular dissatisfaction increased until July 1975, when Gowon was deposed as chief of state in a bloodless coup d'état while attending a conference of African leaders in Uganda. The leader of the coup and the next chief of state, Brigadier Murtala Ramat Muhammed, indicated that he would not depart from the general policies of the Gowon regime but that the nation needed discipline and direction. From Kampala, the capital of Uganda, General Gowon announced his full support of the new regime.

During his short administration, Murtala Muhammed increased the number of states from 12 to 19, made plans to move

Courtesy of Eliot Elisofon, Eliot Elisofon Archives, National Museum of African Art, Smithsonian Institution
A large crowd gathers at a political rally in support of Nnamdi Azikiwe. A leader during the 1940s, Azikiwe spoke against European influence in Africa.

Independent Picture Service

As the civil war progressed, more heavy, complex weapons—such as these tanks and armored personnel carriers—were used.

the federal capital from Lagos to Abuja, got rid of corrupt and incompetent officers in the public service, and set in motion ef-

Independent Picture Service

Sir Ahmadu Bello was a political and religious leader of the former Northern Region. Along with other prominent officials, he was assassinated in a coup d'état in 1966.

forts to reform the local government system. His assassination in an unsuccessful coup attempt in February 1976 did not halt the process of removing the military from politics. The constitutional committee set up by Murtala Muhammed designed a constitutional draft that was approved by the military government and that took effect October 1, 1979.

Under the Constitution of 1979, Nigeria abandoned the British parliamentary system it had inherited from colonial times in favor of an executive presidential system similar to that of the United States. The people elected a president and a bicameral (two-house) national legislature. Alhaji Shehu Shagari was declared the winner of the presidential elections held in 1979 and in 1983. Although Shagari himself was an honest leader, corruption among government officials, along with increased crime and falling oil revenues, led to a coup d'état. On December 31, 1983, the fourth successful military coup in the history of Nigeria toppled the Shagari government and brought Major General Muhammadu Buhari to power. Another coup in 1985 ushered in Major General Ibrahim Babangida to replace Buhari.

Babangida and the military government run by him make all policy decisions and determine all laws. Since each of the 19 states receives most of its revenue from the central government, few regional leaders are willing to challenge Babangida's wishes.

Military Government

The Federal Military Government (FMG) of Nigeria is headed by a Supreme Military Council (SMC), which is composed of 19 members, including General Babangida, the chiefs of the military services, and other military commanders. The SMC makes all policy decisions and enacts all laws. A Federal Executive Council, made up of the head of state, the chief of staff, and 18 federal ministers—of which the majority are civilians—assists the SMC. The National Council of State—a group of 8 of the principal SMC members and the 19 state governors—is responsible for financial, economic, and social decisions affecting the states.

Independent Picture Service

Yakubu Gowon headed Nigeria's federal military government from 1966 to 1975. After the civil war, which ended in 1970, Gowon was unsuccessful in restoring civilian rule to the nation. In July 1975 he was deposed and later found refuge in Great Britain.

Independent Picture Service

Abubakar Tafawa Balewa became Nigeria's first prime minister in 1957 and served in that capacity through independence until his death in 1966 during the military takeover of the government.

Independent Picture Service

During the civil war the Nigerian army regularly informed foreign newspeople about its operations. Here, a colonel shows a map to journalists in Rivers state.

31

Political parties are prohibited, as are virtually all political activities. Human rights are carefully limited. Individuals may be detained by the government without trial for periods of up to three months, which can be renewed indefinitely. The FMG has severely limited the freedom of a historically independent Nigerian press with a decree that makes it illegal to publish anything critical of the government.

After coming to power in 1984, the FMG established military tribunals to try individuals accused of economic mismanagement and corruption under the previous civilian government. The rest of the judicial system remained intact, preserving both federal and state courts as well as a supreme court. The constitution also provides for Islamic and local ethnic laws to be carried out in civil cases.

Nigeria has been divided into 19 states since 1976. This new arrangement broke up the previous four large regions and has succeeded in diluting the rivalry between the north and south. The head of the FMG appoints a military governor for each state. Since its creation, each state has worked toward establishing a distinctive identity as well as a suitable state capital. Individual states have 8 to 12 state ministries, each of which is headed by a commissioner.

Local government bodies play important administrative and judicial roles. They also retain a variety of functions established during the colonial era. Particularly in the northern states, which traditionally have had a centralized government, district leaders and village heads (chiefs) exercise considerable authority.

Independent Picture Service

The City Hall in Lagos, seat of government for about five million urban inhabitants, demonstrates the careful planning that has begun to replace haphazard development in the sprawling capital.

Courtesy of Angene Wilson

Children meet in the center of a village in northern Nigeria. Bicycles and donkeys are still the most common means of transportation.

3) The People

The cultural diversity of Nigeria's 111.9 million people is evident in their various customs, languages, and styles of dress. Estimates vary, but close to 250 separate languages are reported to exist within the borders of Nigeria. Allegiance to family and kinspeople as well as to one's village is very strong, and most Nigerians are proud of their ethnic heritage. The largest groups— in order of decreasing size—are the Hausa, Yoruba, Ibo, and Fulbé.

Hausa

Comprising 21 percent of Nigeria's population, the Hausa live in northern Nigeria and form the largest group in the country. Their language is one of the most widely spoken

33

Independent Picture Service

Members of the Urhobo stilt dancers rehearse for a competition of ethnic dancing to be performed before the queen of Ibadan. These dancers won second prize.

tongues in Africa, since it is used in many regions as the language of commerce. Islam is the dominant religion among the Hausa, and there is an obvious Arabic influence in their culture.

The Hausa have a reputation as astute traders, traveling far and wide to conduct business. They are often found throughout West Africa in the small shops that cater to tourists.

Independent Picture Service

The Efik peoples make their home in southeastern Nigeria, most notably in the port town of Calabar. Here, an Efik man displays an elaborate ceremonial costume.

Independent Picture Service

"Cattle" Fulbé—who follow a traditional, nomadic life-style of livestock herding—travel lightly, often packing only water for a day's work.

Independent Picture Service

A member of a northwestern Nigerian ethnic group wears a distinctive, geometric hairstyle.

Courtesy of United Nations

This Busawa girl was one among thousands of villagers to resettle when homes were submerged by the reservoir of the Kainji Dam.

Courtesy of Eliot Elisofon Archives, National Museum of African Art, Smithsonian Institution

This Yoruba king bears two symbols of authority: a ceremonial fly whisk and a beaded crown. The partial veil of beads is a reminder of the king's once customary isolation from his people. After being crowned, the king traditionally appeared in public only once a year, for the sacrifice to Ogun, the god of iron.

Yoruba

Nigeria's second largest ethnic group, the Yoruba, comprises 20 percent of the population. The Yoruba language is spoken by over 15 million people, primarily in southwestern Nigeria. Like many Nigerian languages, Yoruba is a tonal tongue, which means that the same combination of sounds may have different meanings depending on the tone used in pronunciation. The Yoruba tradition is rich in drama, poetry, and masquerade—a social gathering at which people wear masks and costumes.

The tendency to form associations and secret societies is very strong among the Yoruba. Wherever a large number of Yoruba exist outside their homeland, an organization for their mutual support and common interests will develop. A distinc-

tive blue cloth is often included in the dress of a Yoruba woman. Men still appear in their loose *agbada* (shirt) and folded cap.

Ibo

The Ibo make up 17 percent of Nigeria's people. Most Ibo reside in the southeast, but they have long been spread throughout the nation as shopkeepers, clerks, and government officials. Historically, Ibo society has never been controlled by a central authority. The Ibo were the first ethnic group in Nigeria to embrace Western culture. Thus, during colonial rule they held many important positions in business and government.

Strong traditions of wood carving and pottery exist among the Ibo, and many groups are well known for their music and dance. As is the case with some other groups, elaborate hairstyles for women are believed to enhance beauty and to bring out a youthful appearance. Wrestling is a very popular sport among young Ibo men. Christianity now dominates among the Ibo, but local religions remain strong.

Fulbé

The Fulbé (called the Fulani by the Hausa) have two distinct lifestyles—one that is settled and one that is wandering. "Town" Fulbé are often indistinguishable from the Hausa among whom they live, but "cattle" Fulbé maintain a traditional, independent way of life. Small groups of cattle Fulbé wander the northern countryside selling beef and milk products to villagers and marketing manure to farmers.

Nomadic Fulbé carry a minimum of baggage, using what is available in the savanna wilderness of the north for their encampments and for their daily needs. As the settled population expands and crowds out the Fulbé's grazing grounds, however, the traditional lifestyle of the Fulbé is threatened with extinction. Nevertheless, they make up 9 percent of the population.

Family Life and Marriage

In the extended family of Nigerian society, all kinspeople are treated as close brothers and sisters rather than as distant relatives. This system provides automatic child care for working mothers and single parents, as

Courtesy of Christian Reformed World Relief Committee

Sections of the Fulbé population display strikingly Mediterranean features. The straight profile and the skin tone—the lightest among Nigerians—suggest trans-Saharan or Middle Eastern ancestry.

well as security for the elderly, since the young are expected to care for the old. Hospitality is part of the Nigerian code of ethics. A well-off elder brother may extend hospitality to his younger siblings for many years. Strangers also are treated with great respect and, in most cases, are offered food and lodging.

Marriage customs differ among ethnic groups, but most require that a bride price be paid by the prospective groom. At one time this payment may have been made in cattle or cowrie shells (glossy, brightly colored seashells), but now it is usually settled in currency. The Muslim peoples of the north and west are polygynous—a man may have up to four wives, depending upon his ability to support them.

The rituals that accompany marriage vary greatly, but they usually are spread out over a period of days rather than occurring in the single, brief ceremony common to Western nations. Many urban Nigerians have taken up the Western custom of a church wedding, complete with white veils and the traditional cake. As elsewhere in the world, a wedding is an occasion for feasting and dancing, and the extravagance of the celebration is a sign of the family's wealth.

Religion

Religion occupies a central place in the lives of most people in Nigeria. Often Nigerians have an individual approach to religion, combining elements from more than one tradition into a unique blend, suited to their own spiritual needs.

ISLAM

Approximately 47 percent of Nigerians are Muslim. Islamic religious practices are strictly followed in the north, although in remote areas practices may be less traditional. Each day devout Muslim men can be seen facing Mecca—the Islamic holy city in Saudi Arabia—in prayer. At midday on Fridays most men attend prayers at the central mosque. Even the trains may stop at prayer time. The requirement for almsgiving (charitable donations) supports large numbers of blind people as well as handicapped beggars in the towns.

The Islamic title of *alhaji*—one who has made the hajj (pilgrimage) to Mecca—is held in great respect. A greater number of pilgrims are able to make this journey now that airplanes have largely replaced overland caravans as the chief means of transportation to Mecca.

Independent Picture Service

A mosque graces the old section of Kano. Not all African mosques duplicate this traditional style. In Burkina Faso, they may be tall hives of hand-smoothed, baked earth.

Independent Picture Service

Nigerians practice diverse religions. An emir *(above),* or chief, confers with an imam, or Muslim leader, during a mass meeting. A Christian church *(left)* in Ondo state reflects European influences. Hausa drummers *(below)* perform on "talking drums" to celebrate weddings, the naming of newborns, and the arrival of important people.

Photo by Jim Hathaway

Independent Picture Service

CHRISTIANITY

Christianity has had a profound impact on Nigerian society, most notably in the south and on the Jos Plateau. As in other parts of the continent, Christian churches are growing rapidly, and 34 percent of the population now practices Christianity.

During the nineteenth and much of the twentieth centuries, Christian missionary agencies established hospitals and clinics, led campaigns that improved literacy, and ran schools that trained many of the country's early leaders. A substantial foreign Christian community still exists in a few places—in Jos, for example—but most of the affairs of Nigerian churches are now in the hands of a Nigerian clergy.

Some of the most remarkable growth in Christianity has occurred within the African church movement. In many cases, Nigerians have established their own versions of Christian churches that are free of some of the cultural influences of Europeans. The Cherubim and Seraphim movement, for example, has spread rapidly and now numbers over 2,000 churches.

Courtesy of Eliot Elisofon, Eliot Elisofon Archives, National Museum of African Art, Smithsonian Institution

A Muslim minaret—which is derived from the Arabic word *manarah,* or lighthouse—has balconies from which the muezzin, or crier, summons the faithful to prayer.

NIGERIAN RELIGIONS

Nigeria has an extremely rich tradition in local religious beliefs, rites, and practices. Many Nigerian antiques and artifacts are ritual objects that were used in religious services. Nigerian religions use objects made from carved wood and other materials to represent spiritual forces. All but the most orthodox Muslim and Christian Nigerians continue to observe some of the traditional religious practices of the country.

Traditionally, a supreme being existed for each ethnic group. The Yoruba called their highest god Olorun; to the Ibo she was Ala (earth mother). Lesser gods, such as Ogun (the Yoruba god of war) and Sango (the Yoruba god of thunder), had their own shrines. Spirits—who were embodied in specific ancestors, in persons associated with local places, or in natural features—occupied the lowest rank. Some people believe they can master these spirits by correct invocations and charms.

Independent Picture Service

A masquerade dancer performs in Cross River state. Traditional rituals using masks to represent the spirits are still conducted among some groups, especially in more remote areas.

Food

Meals are not a formality in Nigeria, and family members do not necessarily dine together. For the typical Nigerian, food is eaten to sustain the body and is not considered a social event or a form of entertainment.

Characteristic Nigerian foods vary among regions and groups, but some are eaten nationwide. *Tuwo* and *miya* are staple dishes in the north. They consist of a firm dumpling made from ground sorghum or millet that is dipped into a spicy sauce. *Gari*, or cassava flour, was once used only in the south, but now it is a staple throughout the country. A great deal of time and care goes into the preparation of soups and sauces. For example, *egusi* soup is a high-protein blend of ground egusi and melon seeds seasoned with pepper and fish, shellfish, or meat. *Fufu*, made from pounded yams, is heavy

Photo by Phil Porter

Grains such as millet and sorghum appear in numerous Nigerian dishes. *Tuwo*, a national specialty, combines sorghum dumplings with a pepper sauce.

Courtesy of Eliot Elisofon, Eliot Elisofon Archives, National Museum of African Art, Smithsonian Institution

Women and children spend a portion of their day sorting kola nuts, which eventually find their way into Western soft drinks.

Bamboo screens, squared off into a cage, help this fisherman increase his catch.

Courtesy of FAO

and filling. In coastal areas, fish is very popular. Citrus fruits, mangoes, bananas, and pineapples abound.

In urban areas, many families have adopted the beefsteak and potatoes of Western cuisine. Numerous restaurants can be found whose specialties range from the standard rice and sauce or peppered chicken to more exotic dishes. The number of snack foods available in a marketplace is impressive. Although they vary by season, common snacks include sugarcane, roasted maize, pieces of broiled meat on sticks, and bean cakes.

Health

A warm, moist climate provides an atmosphere in which many disease-producing organisms thrive and pose a threat to humans. Public health problems—from debilitating disease to poor nutrition—are a continuing concern in Nigeria. In addition, toxic waste from Europe dumped along Nigeria's coast in the late 1980s posed a further danger to health.

Abundant breeding places exist for the anopheles mosquito—the carrier of malaria. Despite spraying to eradicate these pests and the widespread use of preventive medicines, malaria continues to be a seri-

ous health problem. The tsetse fly, which thrives in the dense undergrowth in southern areas, spreads a blood infection that can lead to sleeping sickness in humans and to nagana in livestock. The tsetse fly is the major reason why horses and cows are relatively scarce in the south.

Independent Picture Service

A Yoruba woman holds her child while waiting her turn at a rural health clinic.

42

Football (soccer) is the most popular sport in Nigeria among both spectators and participants.

Independent Picture Service

Photo by Jim Hathaway

Clean water is crucial in the effort to prevent the spread of tropical diseases. This house has its own miniature water tower, here being refilled from a water tanker.

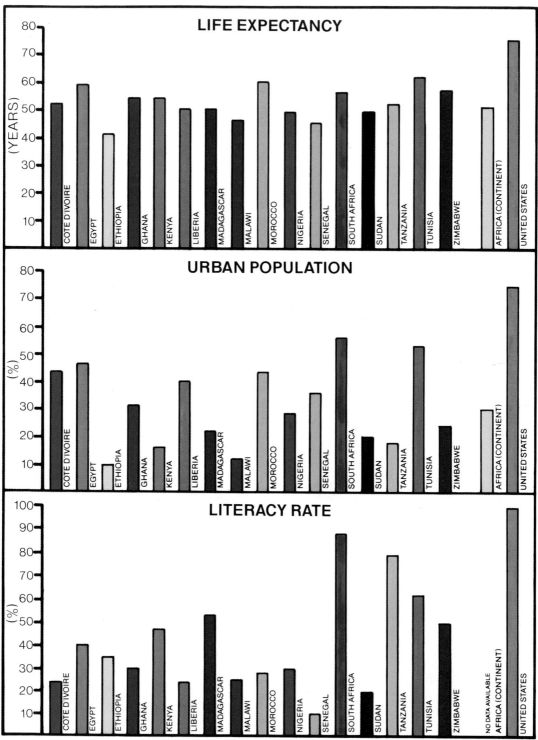

LIFE EXPECTANCY

(YEARS)

COTE D'IVOIRE · EGYPT · ETHIOPIA · GHANA · KENYA · LIBERIA · MADAGASCAR · MALAWI · MOROCCO · NIGERIA · SENEGAL · SOUTH AFRICA · SUDAN · TANZANIA · TUNISIA · ZIMBABWE · AFRICA (CONTINENT) · UNITED STATES

URBAN POPULATION

(%)

COTE D'IVOIRE · EGYPT · ETHIOPIA · GHANA · KENYA · LIBERIA · MADAGASCAR · MALAWI · MOROCCO · NIGERIA · SENEGAL · SOUTH AFRICA · SUDAN · TANZANIA · TUNISIA · ZIMBABWE · AFRICA (CONTINENT) · UNITED STATES

LITERACY RATE

(%)

COTE D'IVOIRE · EGYPT · ETHIOPIA · GHANA · KENYA · LIBERIA · MADAGASCAR · MALAWI · MOROCCO · NIGERIA · SENEGAL · SOUTH AFRICA · SUDAN · TANZANIA · TUNISIA · ZIMBABWE · NO DATA AVAILABLE AFRICA (CONTINENT) · UNITED STATES

Artwork by Jim Simondet

The three factors depicted in this graph suggest differences in the quality of life among 16 African nations. Averages for the United States and the entire continent of Africa are included for comparison. Data taken from "1987 World Population Data Sheet" and *PC-Globe*.

Early deaths from these and other diseases, along with a population that is expected to double in 24 years, have contributed to a very high percentage of young people in Nigeria. Forty-five percent of the nation's people are under age 15, and only 2 percent are 65 or older. Although these statistics are average for Africa, they contrast sharply to the Western world, where about 21 percent are under age 15 and about 13 percent are over 64. In addition, Nigeria's life expectancy of 47 years of age—again not unusual for an African country—is well below the Western average of about 75 years.

Recreation

Nigerian families spend their leisure time in a variety of ways. Children frequently play singing and clapping games. Groups of people of the same age and sex gather in the evening to converse or to listen to the radio. Many sports are popular, but soccer is the national athletic activity. Field hockey, tennis, basketball, and rugby are played in schools and clubs. Horse racing and polo have a long history in the northern states and are popular spectator sports.

Although only the wealthy own their own televisions, some states have constructed public viewing areas where most of the population of a village may gather for an evening's amusement. In the towns, eager spectators crowd inexpensive open-air cinemas to watch action films from India, China, and the United States. After the cinemas close, people often regroup at beer halls and night clubs. In villages, few of which have such facilities, kerosene lanterns go out quite early at night, since the inhabitants have to get up at sunrise the next day.

Courtesy of Ruth Karl

Ibadan students enjoy walking to school together. Their city boasts Nigeria's oldest postsecondary institution, the University of Ibadan.

Education

In Nigeria education is a national passion. Although Nigerians may speak two or three languages, they often read and write none, causing the nation's literacy rate to be estimated at only 25 to 35 percent. Adult education programs and the introduction of free primary education for children are addressing this problem.

Individual states have begun to expand secondary education and teacher-training institutions. Five federally founded universities—at Lagos, Ibadan, Zaria, Ife, and Nsukka—provide higher education. In addition to the government institutions —which offer professional, commercial, and vocational training—a host of self-improvement courses provide students with training in specific job skills. The federal

Independent Picture Service

Science courses are an indication of Western influence in Nigeria's schools. At a teachers' college in Lagos, these students work on laboratory experiments for a chemistry class.

Independent Picture Service

At a school for the deaf, an elementary instructor gives a lesson in beginning Yoruba.

Independent Picture Service

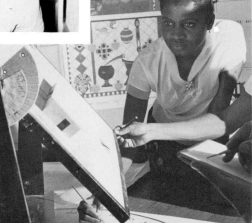

Advanced educational facilities are expanding throughout West Africa. Here, a Nigerian woman uses a technical instrument as part of her architectural course.

46

This Nigerian abstract picture, which is composed of thousands of colored beads, was presented to Princess Anne of Great Britain. Nigeria is a member of the British Commonwealth.

Independent Picture Service

Wole Soyinka, one of Nigeria's most distinguished writers, received the Nobel Prize for literature in 1986. His works include drama, poetry, and fiction. Soyinka also teaches literature at the University of Ibadan.

Courtesy of Nobel Foundation

A member of the Bini ethnic group carved this wooden altar. The Bini share with the Yoruba a reputation for producing fine works of art.

Courtesy of Delmar Lipp, Eliot Elisofon Archives, National Museum of African Art, Smithsonian Institution

government and the states have generous scholarship funds. Nigerian university students can also be found in London, New York, and Los Angeles.

The Arts

Music and dance are important elements in Nigerian life. Traditional instruments—such as drums, flutes, and various stringed instruments—are played in the countryside. City dwellers more commonly hear electric guitars and saxophones.

The traditional activities for visual artists in Nigeria are wood carving and wood sculpture. But Nigerian artists and artisans have also used decorative and symbolic forms in their weaving, pottery, and architecture. Most traditional artistic creations are put to either practical or ceremonial use.

Many Nigerian artists have adopted Western forms, from abstract painting to modern architecture, literature, and drama. Several authors—including Chinua Achebe, Wole Soyinka, and J. P. Clark—have achieved an international reputation. In 1986 Soyinka was the first African to win the Nobel Prize for literature.

Another aspect of Nigerian literature draws on the nation's oral traditions—storytelling, poetry, and proverbs. Unlike European poetry, which is written down and usually read in private, Yoruba poetry is shared at social and ceremonial gatherings.

Independent Picture Service

Major Muslim holidays are celebrated with great zeal in the northern states. At the Islamic festival concluding Ramadan—a 30-day period of fasting and prayer—horse riders wearing their finest dress parade through towns and stage a massive horse charge to salute the ruling nobility.

Independent Picture Service

Independent Picture Service

Ebony and ivory are favored artistic mediums in West Africa, as demonstrated by the sculpted bust *(left)* and the elephant horn trumpet *(right)*.

Although Nigeria was once ranked as a major exporter of peanuts, domestic consumption outstripped production in the 1970s, and peanuts are now imported.

Yosef Hadar/World Bank Photo

4) The Economy

After independence, the Nigerian economy appeared to be doing very well. A remarkable export surplus from the oil boom in the early 1970s resulted in an accumulation of foreign currency. A dramatic shift took place in national production away from agriculture and toward manufacturing, construction, and transport. Social services also began to expand.

Nevertheless, weaknesses and problems exist throughout the economy in the 1980s. The rate of inflation has risen sharply, in part because of the cost of maintaining a 100,000-person army. Widespread unemployment, especially among people who have only a primary-school education, is regarded as one of the most serious economic problems facing the country. Nigeria's total GNP, or gross national product (the total value of goods and services produced in the country), is over $65 billion a year. But the money is divided among a much greater number of people than in other African nations.

Among the priorities that the government has set in its recent National Development Plan are efforts to produce food more cheaply and to improve rural facilities. Goals also include achieving more balanced economic growth, decreasing the rate of unemployment, and converting some privately held economic interests to government control.

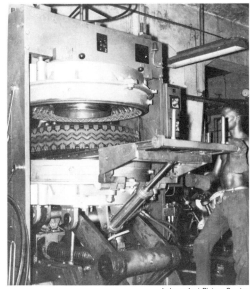

Independent Picture Service

The success of a tire factory in Ikeja reflects the economic shift toward manufacturing and away from agriculture.

Courtesy of Ruth Karl

Traditionally, markets were held only once every four to seven days, according to a cycle that varied from region to region. With the increasing volume of trade, however, transactions in between market days have become more common, and the periodic market has been replaced to some extent by shops that stay open all week.

A village woman gathers the small amount of water that remains in an evaporated pond. A number of serious droughts have been recorded in northern Nigeria during the last 100 years, making water a precious commodity.

Courtesy of CARE

Agriculture

Agriculture traditionally has been the most important sector of Nigeria's economy. Yet its share of the GNP has fallen from more than 60 percent in 1962 to less than 20 percent in 1987. Because rainfall is vital to an agricultural economy, the extreme variability of rain in Nigeria is a serious problem. The total annual rainfall often is adequate for crop growth, but it may be poorly distributed over the growing season. For example, a parched area may suddenly become flooded. Too much or too little water is a common hardship in Nigeria.

In the early 1970s parts of the northern states suffered from the effects of a five-year drought. The drought dominated the entire sub-Saharan zone of Africa from Senegal to Ethiopia—an extreme example of the vulnerability of the environment. The inhabitants of these areas saw their animals and crops perish, and they either existed on relief donations or were forced to emigrate from their homes.

Courtesy of Christian Reformed World Relief Committee

Most of Nigeria's agricultural crops are grown on small family farms, where most farmers grow just enough food to feed their families.

TRADITIONAL AGRICULTURE

About 70 percent of all Nigerians earn their livelihood from farming. Most farms are small and are run by families who use simple production techniques. A wide range of hoes and hand-held plows have been developed to suit various soil types and climatic conditions. Village farmers have occasionally been criticized for their inefficient production, but they have provided the bulk of both export and domestic crops.

Most Nigerian farmers have a system of intercropping in which many crops—sorghum, black-eyed peas, okra, peanuts, and maize, for example—are planted in the

Farmers build silos out of mud and straw to hold grain. Nigeria's principal crops include sorghum, millet, maize, rice, yams, cacao, peanuts, cotton, and palm oil.

Courtesy of FAO

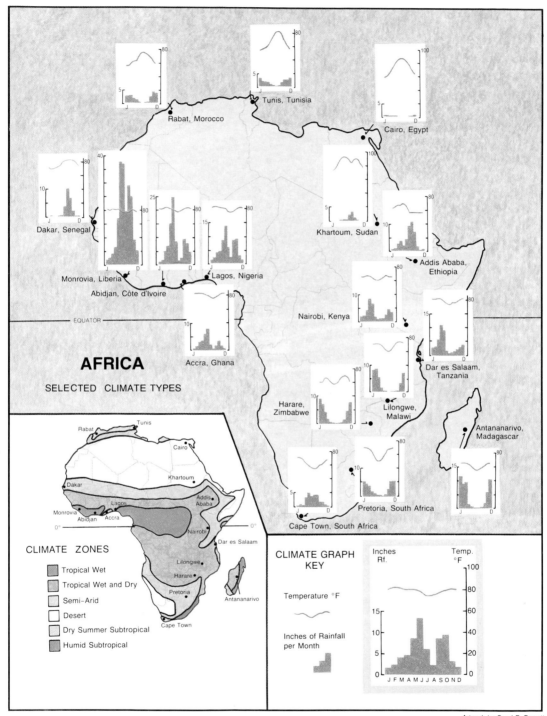

AFRICA

SELECTED CLIMATE TYPES

Rabat, Morocco
Tunis, Tunisia
Cairo, Egypt
Dakar, Senegal
Khartoum, Sudan
Addis Ababa, Ethiopia
Monrovia, Liberia
Abidjan, Côte d'Ivoire
Lagos, Nigeria
Accra, Ghana
Nairobi, Kenya
Dar es Salaam, Tanzania
Harare, Zimbabwe
Lilongwe, Malawi
Antananarivo, Madagascar
Pretoria, South Africa
Cape Town, South Africa

EQUATOR

CLIMATE ZONES

Tropical Wet
Tropical Wet and Dry
Semi-Arid
Desert
Dry Summer Subtropical
Humid Subtropical

CLIMATE GRAPH KEY

Temperature °F

Inches of Rainfall per Month

Inches Rf.
Temp. °F

J F M A M J J A S O N D

Artwork by Carol F. Barrett

These climate graphs show the monthly change in the average rainfall received and in the average temperature from January to December for the capital cities of 16 African nations. On the graph for Lagos, Nigeria, note that the capital has a relatively humid climate—though not as wet as the climate along the eastern border. In Nigeria rainfall amounts diminish from the southern coast to the country's northern boundary. Data taken from *World-Climates* by Willy Rudloff, Stuttgart, 1981.

Photo by Jim Hathaway

Nigerian markets are run almost entirely by women. A tremendous variety of foods are available, including poultry in baskets, yams, and green vegetables. Household goods – such as firewood, soap, and clay pots for cooking or storage – are also at hand.

same plot. In sparsely populated regions, fields are cultivated for five or six years and are then left unused for an equal period. In densely settled areas such as Kano, the same fields are used every year. To maintain soil fertility, farmers add animal manure, household refuse, or commercial fertilizer to the soil.

In most cases, farmers who plant on a small scale are also responsible for the processing and storage of their crops. For example, cacao pods must be split and fermented, coffee beans must be dried and husked, and tobacco must be cured. Food crops are usually stored in simple home granaries, which are jealously guarded

since they may contain a farmer's entire wealth. Because close to 20 percent of the crops produced and stored are destroyed by pests, storage is one of the most serious problems facing farmers.

ATTEMPTS TO IMPROVE AGRICULTURE

Although the nation once exported more food than it imported, Nigeria was forced to buy foreign-produced food to survive during the 1970s and 1980s. Faced with this dangerous state of affairs, the military government launched the Operation Feed the Nation program in 1976. The government also created schemes to develop irrigation and to provide farmers with fertilizer and seed at reduced rates. Farm credit programs and the redistribution of landownership were also attempted to increase large-scale, mechanized farming.

The government of Ibrahim Babangida has begun a reform program that will allow food prices to rise, which will encourage farmers to produce more for export. The reforms penalize the urban elite in favor of farmers, which would be impossible in a nonmilitary, democratic government since political power would be concentrated among city dwellers.

Internal Trade

At the heart of Nigeria's complex and dynamic system of internal trade is the local market. In cities, these markets may be extremely large, with up to 10,000 sellers meeting daily. In rural areas trading is conducted at intervals of four to seven days.

The marketplace serves a number of functions. It is a place of companionship, where traders may dawdle, gossip, and haggle as they please. Operating costs are generally quite low, and a wide variety of goods are available, even in remote locations that can be reached only by bicycle. Women do most of the selling in the southern areas, and some women have become quite wealthy.

The demand for consumer goods in Nigeria is substantial. Even with an average income of less than $20 a month, a Nigerian villager can save for a new tin roof, for example, or even for a wristwatch

World Bank Photo

Agricultural production in Nigeria has grown stronger in the 1980s. In 1986 the World Bank awarded over $200 million in project loans to the agricultural sector, encouraging the nation's growth as a farming country.

or a transistor radio. An expanding middle class of civil servants, teachers, and businesspeople is buying refrigerators, stereos, motorcycles, and television sets. National consumerism, combined with the lively system of domestic commerce, has promoted the growth of many industries.

Small Businesses

Throughout the country, enterprising Nigerians have established small-scale businesses, which they operate alone or with the help of a few employees. Many of these entrepreneurs are farmers who add to their incomes by practicing a trade. Some businesses are based on longstanding craft occupations, such as blacksmithing, tailoring, weaving, pottery making, or leather working.

Other types of craftspeople and businesspeople, however, also have emerged to meet new needs. The sound of motor-powered grinding machines, for example, resounds throughout most villages, for it is much easier to have grain ground for a few pennies than to spend the morning pounding it by hand at home. Service businesses that employ modern skills—such as fur-

Independent Picture Service

Hand weaving is an important small industry. Here, a woman weaves cloth in the characteristic pattern of her ethnic group.

niture manufacturers, automotive garages, and photography studios—have also sprung up.

Industry

After the civil war of the 1960s, output in the industrial sector rose steadily for a number of years. Building and construction more than doubled in the first five years of the 1970s. Demand for building materials far exceeded local supplies, and government import permits often were obtained through corrupt means.

Most of the manufacturing industry in Nigeria is designed to replace imported articles. Of these new businesses, the largest is the textile industry, with 60 factories, most of which are owned jointly by the government and foreign companies. The food industry is quite large and diversified, with breweries, fruit and meat canneries, flour mills, and sugar factories being the most important concerns. A large variety of other consumer industries—which produce tobacco, shoes, detergents, margarine, paint, and cosmetics—also exist. Housewares, pharmaceuticals, and office

Independent Picture Service

A worker attends a machine at a blanket factory in Kano. Nigeria's cotton textile industry began production in 1957.

Courtesy of Marathon Oil Company

Oil rigs rising up through the palms, like this one operated by Marathon Oil Company, saw less activity after the oil boom of the 1970s.

Courtesy of Gulf Oil Corporation

An aerial view depicts the "Key Largo" drilling wells, located off the coast of Nigeria. The large landing pad accommodates helicopters carrying workers, tools, and supplies.

equipment are also manufactured in Nigeria.

Heavy industry became increasingly important in the early 1970s with the development of tire manufacturing, aluminum rolling, tin smelting, petroleum refining, and steel milling. In addition, Peugeot and Volkswagen have built motor vehicle assembly plants in Kaduna and Lagos.

Oil and Energy

With the discovery of oil in the Niger Delta in 1956, Nigeria entered an era of rapid economic growth. The nation quickly became dependent on its earnings from the petroleum industry. By the 1970s petro-leum had replaced agricultural exports as the largest source of foreign revenue and accounted for a fourth of the value of production in the country.

During the 1980s, however, the industry has suffered severe setbacks. An international collapse in oil prices in 1986 brought Nigeria's economic problems to a new crisis level when prices dropped from $25 to $8 a barrel. Experts believe that the oil boom is over, and Nigeria must plan for limited growth, based as much on agriculture as on oil.

Although Nigeria has been exploiting its oil reserves for over 30 years, it has yet to develop other petroleum products in addition to crude oil. The country utilizes

Nigeria's coal deposits are located near Enugu in Anambra state. The coal industry has been operating at a loss since the 1950s, largely because of the heavy cost of rail transport to coastal ports.

Courtesy of Eliot Elisofon Archives, National Museum of African Art, Smithsonian Institution

Courtesy of United Nations

The Kainji Dam regulates the flow of the Niger River and generates hydroelectric power. The dam was completed in 1968 and is Nigeria's chief energy source.

little of its natural gas reserves for domestic energy use and less still for export. Nigeria is seeking international energy firms to join in the development of a petrochemicals complex where chemicals would be derived from oil and natural gas. Several plans to develop alternative sources of power—including hydroelectric power as well as gas—are nearly complete, but it may be several years before Nigeria can work out the financial snags and can complete the projects.

Transportation

Nigerians are exceptionally mobile—they have long been accustomed to long-distance travel for trade, visiting, and employment. By the early 1970s Nigeria had one of the best developed communications and transportation networks in Africa, with 2,180 miles of railways and 50,000 miles of roads.

The country's main rail lines run from north to south bringing produce from the interior to the ports and hauling imports inland for distribution. The rail network is operated by the state-owned Nigerian Railway Corporation and, despite active competition from road transport, plays a vital role in the nation's commerce. Passenger traffic on the railroads, however, has declined drastically in recent years because service has grown less dependable.

Road transport dominates Nigeria's interstate commerce. Over 10,000 miles of new roads have been constructed recently. The old trucks that once dominated

Many Nigerians enjoy the convenience of motorbikes and bicycles, especially for travel on dirt roads.

Independent Picture Service

Courtesy of CARE

Nigeria and CARE joined forces in the building of village access roads and similar transportation links. The Aboyne Bridge —shown here under construction—now connects access roads on either side of the Aboyne River.

Photo by Jim Hathaway

Since no bridge is available, passengers wait for the river ferry at Igbokoda, located about 90 miles east of Lagos, to carry them across the waterway. In the past, a string of settlements arose along the edges of rivers where steamer service was provided. Some of these towns, which were called ferry points, disappeared, but others still exist.

Photo by Jim Hathaway

A billboard designed by the government urges travelers on the highway to "export for survival."

passenger travel are rapidly being replaced by fast minibuses and luxury coaches.

Nigeria's principal seaports are Lagos, Warri, Port Harcourt, and Calabar. Since the volume of shipping is so heavy, traffic at these ports is subject to frequent congestion and delays. The 5,331 miles of navigable inland waterways, which primarily consist of the Niger and Benue rivers and their tributaries, constitute an extensive and important part of the transportation system.

Nigeria Airways operates regular international jet service to major European capitals as well as to the United States. It also competes with private airlines in an extensive air network within the country. A number of other international carriers fly to Lagos and Kano.

Goods and people in Nigeria usually rely on means of transportation that are less advanced than jets and oil tankers. Small loads being carried for short distances are usually balanced on the head. Bicycles and motorbikes are seen everywhere, as are donkeys—a dependable, though slower, means of transport.

The Future

The FMG (Federal Military Government) under Major General Babangida has taken steps to improve Nigeria's economy. High priority has been given to developing agriculture, water resources, and the steel and petroleum industries. Legislation has been passed to reduce the level of imports and to encourage and protect domestic industries. Nevertheless, the state of the economy is far from healthy, and major shortages in replacement parts and raw materials continue to force many industries to close.

Despite these pressing economic problems, Babangida has not shied away from the question of Nigeria's political future. The general has pledged to restore civilian rule in 1990. In the meantime he has appointed a committee to seek opinions throughout the country on the principles that should guide Nigeria's future.

Although this debate has opened up longstanding ethnic and religious clashes, it has also been seen as one of several indicators of a new Babangida-style, military democracy. If the search for an acceptable form of government is successful, perhaps Nigerians will at last be able to work together to achieve the stability the nation has been striving for since its independence in 1960.

Photo by Jim Hathaway

These young schoolchildren are among the more than 11 million pupils enrolled each year in primary schools since the early 1980s. They will enjoy a higher literacy rate than previous generations of Nigerians.

Index

17463